T0308487

PIONEER EDITION

By Nancy-Jo Hereford

CONTENTS

Voices
for
Justice

By Nancy-Jo Hereford

Dr. Martin Luther King Jr. speaks to news reporters. Television news helped people learn about the civil rights movement.

OUR WORLD is filled with different forms of media. There are printed materials and photographs. There is television and the Internet. Together, they help us have fun and learn. They help us communicate with others.

People have also used media in another way. Think about it. Where would America be without documents about liberty? How do photos tell stories about human rights? How do television images help to fight injustice? How has social media become a force for freedom?

Discover how media, in one form or another form, has always been a voice for justice.

Lᴇᴛ'ꜱ ꜱᴛᴀʀᴛ ᴡɪᴛʜ the American Revolution. Patriots gave public speeches. They also spread ideas by printing them in pamphlets.

A pamphlet is like a short book. The most famous pamphlet is *Common Sense* by Thomas Paine. It appeared in January 1776. That was seven months before the *Declaration of Independence*. Paine explained why it made sense for America to become independent. He blamed the English king for treating the colonies unfairly.

More than 100,000 copies of *Common Sense* were printed. Many colonists read Paine's ideas. It's a big leap to imagine creating your own country. *Common Sense* helped many colonists to make that leap.

So political pamphlets like *Common Sense* were a voice for justice. They gave Americans good reasons to fight for independence.

Thomas Paine wrote many pamphlets. He urged people to keep fighting for independence.

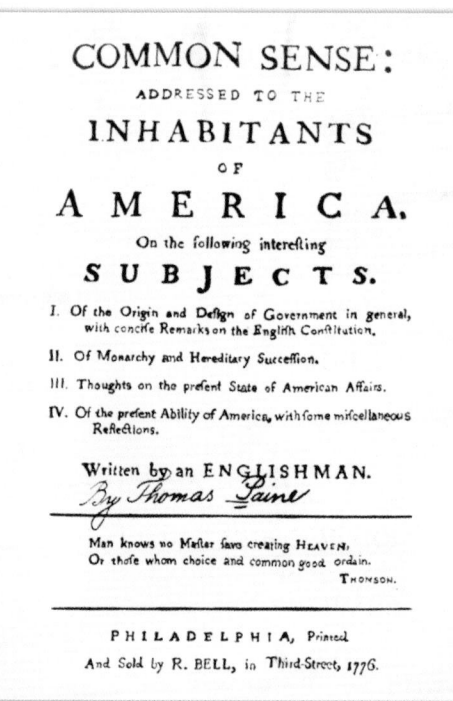

Common Sense *explained why Americans should be independent.*

4

Frederick Douglass described the evils of slavery in his newspaper The North Star.

William Lloyd Garrison disliked the Constitution. Why? Because it did not ban slavery!

Media: Abolitionist Newspapers
THE FREEDOM PRESS

THE AMERICAN REVOLUTION was a success. The United States became independent. But there was not freedom for all. Slavery was still allowed in the new nation.

Slowly, states in the North did away with slavery. Then a **movement** began to abolish, or end, enslavement everywhere in the country.

Some leaders of the anti-slavery movement created newspapers. They printed articles about the cruel treatment of enslaved people. They wrote about why slavery was wrong. *The Liberator* was one of the best-known abolitionist newspapers.

Its founder was William Lloyd Garrison. He published his newspaper for 34 years. He only stopped when the 13th Amendment ended slavery in 1865.

So newspapers were a voice for justice. Over many years, they kept the goal of freedom for enslaved people in the public eye. They helped bring about a United States where there is liberty for all races.

This photograph shows the 1913 march in Washington, D.C. More than 5,000 women joined the parade.

Media: Photographs
WOMEN ON THE MARCH

LET'S RETURN TO America's beginning. There are many well-known Founding Fathers. But there are hardly any famous Founding Mothers. Why? The Constitution did not give women the **right** to vote. In that time, women did not have the same rights as men.

In the 1800s, women started to demand suffrage, or voting rights. It took 72 years for women to win the right to vote.

During those years, camera technology improved. By the late 1800s, photos could be printed in newspapers. Also, women wanted to get more attention for voting rights.

Newspaper photos helped women get attention for their **cause**. They protested in city streets. They marched outside the White House. Photographers captured those events for the newspapers.

The most famous suffrage march took place in Washington, D.C., in 1913. A crowd of men tried to stop the march. Women were injured. Photos of the march changed some people's minds. They began to help the women.

So photos were a voice for justice. Those photos helped women show they wanted a say in government. In 1920, the 19th Amendment gave all women the right to vote.

IT MAY SEEM like television has been around forever. But it's not even 100 years old. People began buying televisions around 1950. By 1960, 90 percent of homes had a TV. It was a new experience to get the news on television. People could see national events in their own living rooms.

Starting in the mid-1950s, television news reported on African Americans protesting for civil rights. Some scenes were inspiring, such as hundreds of peaceful marchers gathering together.

Many people watched Dr. Martin Luther King Jr.'s speeches on television.

Many other scenes were ugly and violent. Viewers saw white adults screaming at black children trying to attend all-white schools. They saw helpless protesters being attacked.

Remember the newspapers that told people about the evils of slavery? Television did something similar. It showed injustices that black Americans lived with.

So television news about civil rights was a voice for justice. Television helped turn public opinion in favor of new laws in the 1960s. Those laws gave equal rights to people of all races.

SOME NEWS PROGRAMS, like the evening news, report information. Another kind of news program, called a documentary, has a different goal. It documents, or tells, about a subject. But it shows real events in a way that supports a particular point of view. It also tries to make viewers care about that subject. Often it uncovers a hidden injustice.

One television documentary made history. It was broadcast the day after Thanksgiving in 1960. By then most families had a television. Viewers of the documentary called "Harvest of Shame" learned about migrant workers in Florida. Migrant workers go from farm to farm picking crops. The documentary showed that these workers were treated unfairly. They barely made enough money to live.

"Harvest of Shame" upset many viewers. They demanded help for these farm laborers. In 1962, Congress passed a law to give migrant workers services, such as health care.

So a documentary is another voice for justice. A good documentary makes people think. Even better, it prompts them to take action.

Now and in the Future

FAST-FORWARD to today. People still learn about problems from printed materials and photos. Television and documentaries are still weapons that fight injustice. What other types of **media** can you name? Keep your eyes and ears open for new kinds of media that are a voice for justice!

Wordwise

cause: an aim that some people support or fight for

media: ways to communicate with a wide audience, like newspapers, magazines, radio, and television

movement: people with the same beliefs or ideas who work together for change

right: a thing you are allowed to do by law

How to Read a Web Page

Where do *you* go first to get information? Chances are it's the Internet. You can find thousands of Web pages about different causes for social justice.

Anyone can create a Web page to support a cause. So how do you know if you can trust the information on a page? You need to use critical thinking. Test your skills. Read this imaginary Web page from a social justice group. Decide if you want to learn more about this group.

Name: *Who is this group? What can you tell about them?*

URL: *Where is the group from? Is it part of a university? Is it part of the government?*

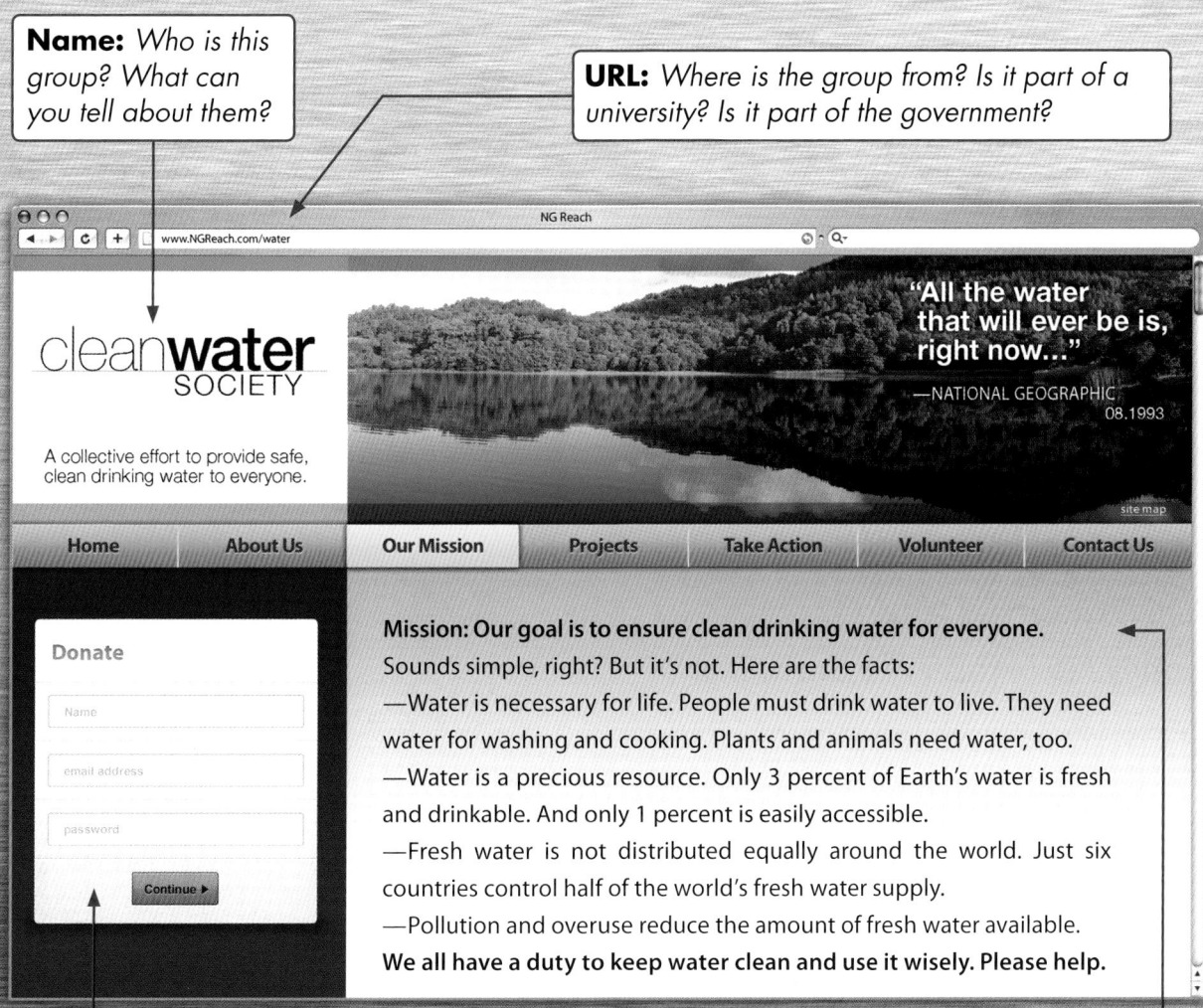

Donation link: *If people give money, how will it be used?*

Mission: *Do you understand what this group is trying to do? Do you agree with its goals?*

Friending
JUSTICE

TAKE A LOOK
AT JUSTICE
IN THE 21ST
CENTURY.

"Tweeting" Revolution

Social media has changed how
people stay in touch in the 21st
century. They talk, text, and send
photos with cell phones. They
post videos on the Internet or visit
personal Web pages. They follow the
"tweets" of pals and even celebrities.

Revolutionary Media

Social media was developed for
communication. It lets people stay in
contact all the time. These qualities
make social media revolutionary.
In some places in the world, social
media is spreading revolution, too.

One way unfair leaders stay in
power is by controlling what people
know. Social media helps people tell
the truth about problems. Protest
leaders can post news or photos on a
Web page seconds after it happens.
They can "tweet" thousands at once
with critical information.

A woman waves the flag of Egypt. Notice the people taking photos with their cell phones.

Protesting Online and in the Street

A revolution in Egypt in 2011 is an example of the impact of social media. President Hosni Mubarak ruled Egypt for 30 years. His government tried to stop dissent, or disagreement.

Through social media, more Egyptians could share their views. One group, called the April 6 Youth Movement, created a Web page. It was used to organize protests. In time, protests brought together citizens of all ages.

"Tweets" and texting helped keep information flowing. Egyptians demanded a new leader. President Mubarak had to step down.

Printed Pages to Texted "Tweets"

People who fight for justice are resourceful. They find tools to fight wrong-doing. They find ways to support fairness. From printed pages to texted "tweets," media has always been a friend to justice.

MediaMessages

Get the message. Then answer these
questions about media and justice.

1 How did people share ideas during
the American Revolution?

2 Why was photography important for
the women's suffrage movement?

3 What is a documentary? How is it
different from the evening news?

4 List two things to pay attention to
when you look at a Web page.

5 How are the ways people use
media to spread social justice today
different from in the past?